25 words

Benchmark
Reading

Starter
2

Benchmark EDUCATION
Building Literacy and Language for Life ™

Introduction

Word Chant

This helps learners become familiar with the key words.

Phonics

This helps learners focus on a special sound.

Get Ready

This section introduces the content of the unit with a related picture and a question to stimulate learners' interest.

Key Words

This section introduces the unit's key words.

Sight Words

This section provides words that learners should be familiar with and able to read.

Reading Passage

The reading passage presents various fiction and nonfiction texts with illustrations and pictures.

Focus

This question helps learners know what to focus on while reading.

Check

Learners can quickly check their understanding.

Story Song

Learners can enhance their reading and speaking skills with the story song.

Find & Draw

Learners can find the unit's sight words in the reading passage.

Phonics Chant

Learners can learn the sounds of letters.

Write & Read / Read & Circle

Learners can practice writing or reading the sounds of letters.

Build Language

This section presents the main sentence pattern in the passage with the chant. Learners can also practice the sentence pattern by tracing the sentence.

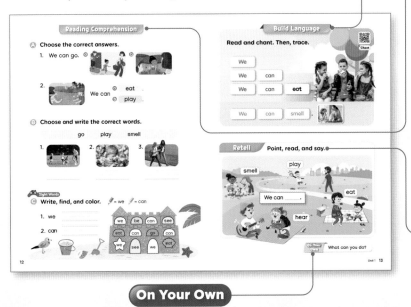

Reading Comprehension

Ⓐ This section provides reading comprehension questions. Learners can check how well they understand the passage by solving questions.

Ⓑ Learners can practice reading and writing the unit's key words.

Ⓒ Learners can practice reading and writing the unit's sight words.

Retell

Learners can retell the passage by pointing at or numbering the pictures.

On Your Own

This section allows learners to think about their own experiences with the unit's topic.

Workbook

The workbook enables learners to review the entire unit through three sections.
• Vocabulary Practice: Learners can review the key words, phonics words, and sight words in the unit.
• Sentence Practice: Learners can practice reading and writing sentences from the passage.
• Reading Practice: Learners can check how well they understand the passage.

Scope and Sequence

My Senses

Unit	Title	Subject	Genre
1	We Can Be Together	Physical Education	Fiction
2	The Parade	Social Studies	Fiction
3	I Can Smell	Science	Nonfiction

We Get Along

Unit	Title	Subject	Genre
4	My Birthday	Social Studies	Fiction
5	We Are Friends	Social Studies	Nonfiction
6	My Mittens	Math	Fiction

Animals

Unit	Title	Subject	Genre
7	My Little Cat	Physical Education	Fiction
8	Animals at Home	Science	Nonfiction
9	Zoo Animals	Science	Fiction

Safety and Transportation

Unit	Title	Subject	Genre
10	We Are Going Home	Literature	Fiction
11	Ready to Play	Physical Education	Fiction
12	Safety Posters	Art	Nonfiction

Key Words	Phonics	Build Language	Page
go, hear, eat, smell, play	sm**ell**, tog**e**ther	**We can** eat.	6
parade, drum, horn, clown, truck	dr**u**m, f**u**n	**I hear** the drums.	14
flower, soap, pizza, sock, trash	tr**a**sh, b**a**d	**I can smell** this flower.	22

Key Words	Phonics	Build Language	Page
balloon, candle, bow, friend, birthday	**b**ow, **b**ox	**I like** the balloon.	30
sing, swing, read, paint, cook	s**ing**, sw**ing**	**We ride** together.	38
dot, stripe, fur, hole, same	**st**ripe, **st**ar	**My mittens have** stripes.	46

Key Words	Phonics	Build Language	Page
run, climb, walk, jump, sleep	**c**at, **c**limb	**I sleep** with my cat.	54
bird, rabbit, crab, fox, fish	**f**ox, **f**ish	**The bird is** at home.	62
giraffe, tall, bear, snake, squirrel	t**all**, sm**all**	**These are** giraffes.	70

Key Words	Phonics	Build Language	Page
way, bus, subway, plane, ship	**w**e, **w**ay	**We are** on the bus.	78
glove, catch, tube, skate, ski	**sk**ate, **sk**i	Take the goggles. **Let's ski**.	86
poster, kitchen, bathroom, bedroom, hall	bedr**oo**m, sch**oo**l	**I put it** in the kitchen.	94

Physical Education

1

Phonics: short e
smell, together

We Can Be Together

Get Ready What are the boys doing?

My Senses

Key Words

A **Listen and repeat the words.**

♫ Word Chant

go

hear

eat

smell

play

Sight Words

we, can

B **Check the correct words.**

1.
☐ hear
☐ play

2.
☐ go
☐ eat

We Can Be Together

26 words

We can go.

We can see.

We can hear.

Story Song

We can eat.

Check

What can they hear?

We can smell.

We can play.

Check

They are a family. [Yes] [No]

We can be together.
We love our family.

Read and color!

1 2 3

Find & Draw

we = ☆
can = △

Ee **Phonics Chant**

e e e smell
e e e together
smell smell smell
together together together

Write & Read

 sm__ll

 tog__ther

Unit 1 **11**

A Choose the correct answers.

1. We can go. ⓐ  ⓑ

2.  We can
   ⓐ eat .
   ⓑ play .

B Choose and write the correct words.

go   play   smell

1.

2.

3.

Sight Words

C Write, find, and color. = we = can

1. we

2. can

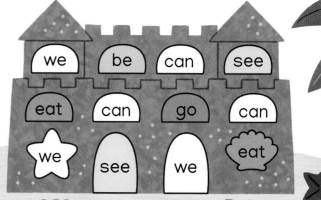

Read and chant. Then, trace.

We

We can

We can eat.

We can smell.

♪ Chant

Retell Point, read, and say.

smell

play

eat

We can _____.

hear

On Your Own What can you do?

The Parade

Get Ready What do you see in the parade?

My Senses

♪ Word **Chant**

A **Listen and repeat the words.**

parade

drum

horn

clown

truck

Sight Words

see, hear

B **Circle the correct words.**

1.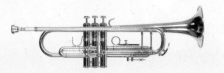

drum | horn

2.

clown | truck

The Parade

25 words

I see the parade.

I hear the drums.

♪ Story Song

I hear the horns.

Check

Who plays the drum?

I see the clowns.

I hear the big truck.

Check

The children hear the big truck. [Yes] [No]

Find & Draw
see = ♡
hear = ◇

The parade is fun.

Uu **Phonics Chant**

u u u drum
u u u fun
drum drum drum
fun fun fun

Read & Circle

u

clown

fun

drum

A **Choose the correct answers.**

1.

I see the _____.

ⓐ clowns   ⓑ horns

2.

I hear the drums. (Yes) (No)

B **Choose and write the correct words.**

1.

| parade |
| fun |

_____
- - - - - - - - -
_____

2.

| horn |
| drum |

_____
- - - - - - - - -
_____

3.

| truck |
| clown |

_____
- - - - - - - - -
_____

Sight Words

C **Write, find, and count.**

1. see - - - - - - - - - ☐

2. hear - - - - - - - - - ☐

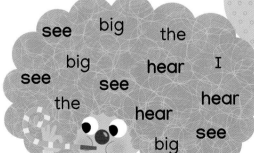

see big the
big hear I
see see
the hear hear
big see
big

Read and chant. Then, trace.

Chant

I

I hear

I hear the drums .

I hear the horns .

Number, read, and say.

① truck   ② drums   ③ horns

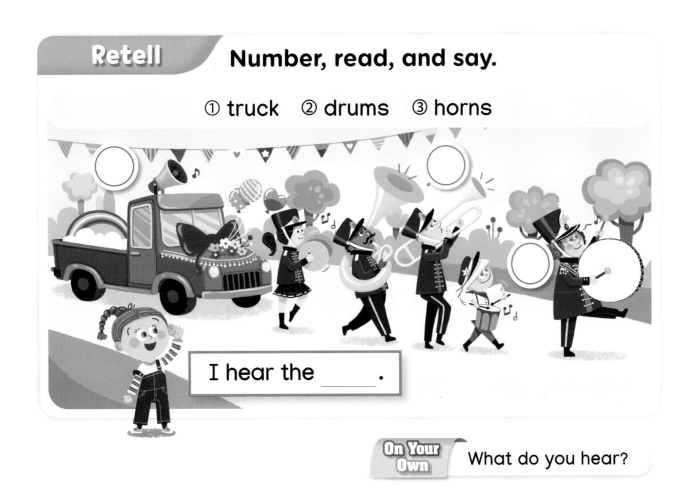

I hear the ____ .

On Your Own   What do you hear?

I Can Smell

My Senses

Get Ready · What does the girl have?

22

🎵 Word Chant

A Listen and repeat the words.

flower

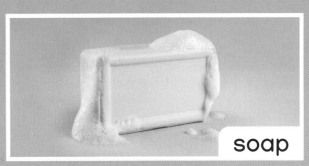
soap

pizza

sock

trash

👀 Sight Words

smell, this

B Check the correct words.

1.
☐ soap
☐ flower

2.
☐ sock
☐ pizza

I Can Smell

31 words

I can smell this flower.

I can smell this soap.

I can smell this pizza.

It smells good.

Check

The pizza smells good.   Yes   No

I can smell this sock.

Check

Who smells the sock?

I can smell this trash.

It smells bad.

Find & Draw

smell = ○
this = ▢

Aa | **Phonics Chant**

a a a trash
a a a bad
trash trash trash
bad bad bad

Write & Read

 tr__sh

 b__d

Reading Comprehension

A Choose the correct answers.

1.
   ⓐ I can smell this soap.
   ⓑ I can smell this pizza.

2.
   I can smell this trash.
   It smells _____.
   ⓐ good   ⓑ bad

B Write the correct words.

1.
   saop

2.
   trsah

3.
   pizaz

 Sight Words

C Write, find, and circle.

1. smell _____

2. this _____

o	s	w	d	t	h	i	s
t	m	s	m	e	l	l	k
h	e	a	s	m	e	l	l
i	l	u	i	a	t	o	c
s	l	v	t	h	i	s	o

28

Read and chant. Then, trace.

I

I | can | smell

I | can | smell | **this flower** .

I | can | smell | this soap .

Retell **Point, read, and say.**

trash

pizza

I can smell this ____ .

flower

sock

On Your Own What can you smell?

My Birthday

Get Ready **What special day is it?**

We Get Along

♪ **Word Chant**

A **Listen and repeat the words.**

balloon

candle

bow

friend

birthday

👓 **Sight Words**

I, like

B **Circle the correct words.**

1.

| balloon | candle |

2.

| bow | friend |

My Birthday

28 words

Focus

What does the boy like?

I like the balloon.

I like the candle.

I like the bow.

Check

Who likes the candle?

I open the box.

I like the boat.

Check

The boy likes the boat. Yes No

Find & Draw

I = ☆
like = △

I like my friends.
What a happy birthday!

Bb

b b b bow
b b b box
bow bow bow
box box box

Read & Circle

b

bow

candle

box

Reading Comprehension

A Choose the correct answers.

1. I open the box.

2.  I like
   ⓐ the balloon .
   ⓑ my friends .

B Choose and write the correct words.

friends	balloon	birthday

1. _____
   _____

2. _____
   _____

3. _____
   _____

C Write, find, and color. 🖊 = I   🖊 = like

1. I _____

2. like _____

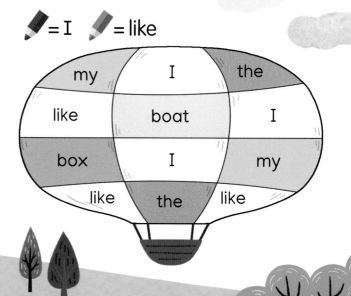

36

Read and chant. Then, trace.

| I | | |
| I | like | |
| I | like | the balloon | .
| I | like | the candle | .

Chant

Retell   Number, read, and say.

① balloon   ② candle   ③ bow   ④ boat

I like the _____ .

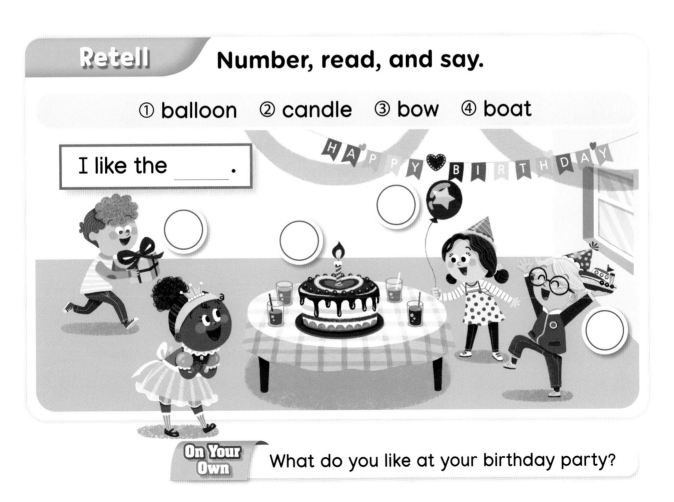

On Your Own   What do you like at your birthday party?

5

We Are Friends

Get Ready What are the girls doing?

We Get Along

♫ Word Chant

A **Listen and repeat the words.**

sing

swing

read

paint

cook

Sight Words

are, together

B **Check the correct words.**

1.
☐ read
☐ sing

2.
☐ paint
☐ cook

We Are Friends

27 words

Focus
What do the children do together?

We are friends.

We sing together.

40

We swing together.

We read together.

Check

Where do they swing?

We are friends.
We paint together.

We cook together.

Check

They are happy. [Yes] [No]

We ride together.
We are happy.

Find & Draw
are = ♡
together = ◇

 ing | **Phonics Chant**

ing ing ing sing
ing ing ing swing
sing sing sing
swing swing swing

Write & Read

 s__ __ __

 sw__ __ __

Reading Comprehension

A **Choose the correct answers.**

1.

   We _____ together.

   ⓐ sing   ⓑ paint

2.

   We ride together.   [Yes]   [No]

B **Choose and write the correct words.**

1.

   read

   swing

   _____
   _____

2.

   sing

   ride

   _____
   _____

3.

   paint

   cook

   _____
   _____

 **Sight Words**

C **Write, find, and count.**

1. are   _____ _____ ☐

2. together   _____ _____ ☐

together
we   are
we
cook
together   together
are   we
are
are
cook

Read and chant. Then, trace.

♪ Chant

We

We | ride

We | ride | together .

We | swing | together .

Retell — Point, read, and say.

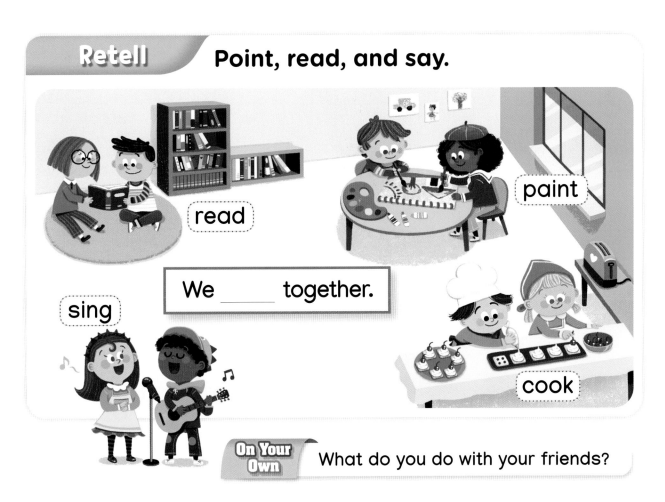

read

paint

We _____ together.

sing

cook

On Your Own — What do you do with your friends?

6

Phonics: st
stripe, star

My Mittens

Get Ready What is the girl wearing?

We Get Along

A Listen and repeat the words.

♪ Word Chant

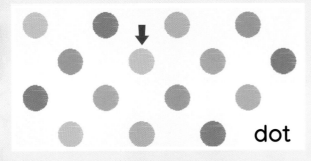
dot

stripe

fur

hole

same

Sight Words

my, have

B Circle the correct words.

1.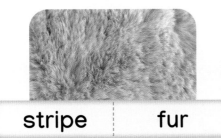

stripe	fur

2.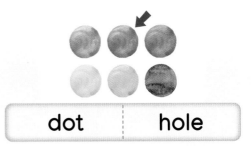

dot	hole

My
Mittens

29 words

What do the children have?

My mittens have dots.

My mittens have stripes.

♪ Story Song

My mittens have fur.

Check

Who has fur mittens?

☐ 　　☐

My mittens have stars.

My mittens have holes.

Check

The boy has holes in his mittens. [Yes] [No]

Look at the snowman.
We have the **same** mitten.

Find & Draw

my = ○
have = ▢

st

Phonics Chant

st st st stripe
st st st star
stripe stripe stripe
star star star

Read & Circle

st

dot

stripe

star

A **Choose the correct answers.**

1.
   ⓐ My mittens have dots.
   ⓑ My mittens have stars.

2.
   Look at the snowman. We have the same _____.
   ⓐ mitten   ⓑ hat

B **Write the correct words.**

1.
   s t r p i e
   _____
   - - - - - - - - - - - -

2.
   h l o e
   _____
   - - - - - - - - - - - -

3. s a e m
   _____
   - - - - - - - - - - - -

 **Sight Words**

C **Write, find, and circle.**

1. my   _____

2. have   _____

Read and chant. Then, trace.

Chant

My mittens

My mittens have

My mittens have **stripes** .

My mittens have fur .

Retell   Number, read, and say.

① stars   ② holes   ③ stripes   ④ dots

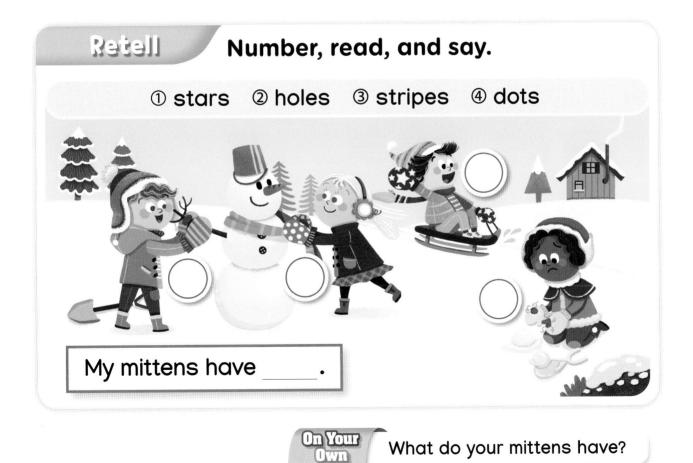

My mittens have _____ .

On Your Own   What do your mittens have?

Physical Education

7

Phonics: c
cat, climb

My Little Cat

Get Ready · Who is on the sofa?

Animals

A **Listen and repeat the words.**

 ♪ Word Chant

run

climb

walk

jump

sleep

Sight Words

with, cat
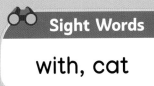

B **Check the correct words.**

1.
   ☐ sleep
   ☐ walk

2.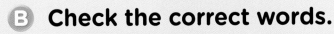
   ☐ run
   ☐ climb

My Little Cat

28 words

· Focus ·

What does the girl do with her cat?

I run with my cat.

I **climb** with my cat.

Story Song

I **walk** with my cat.

Check

Who climbs with the cat?

I jump with my cat.

Cc **Phonics Chant**

c c c cat
c c c climb
cat cat cat
climb climb climb

Write & Read

__at

__limb

Find & Draw

with = ☆
cat = △

I sleep with my cat.
Good night, Kitty!

Check

She sleeps with her dog. [Yes] [No]

Reading Comprehension

A **Choose the correct answers.**

1. I jump with my cat.

 ⓐ  ⓑ

2.

I ⓐ run / ⓑ sleep with my cat.

B **Choose and write the correct words.**

climb   jump   walk

1. _____

2. _____

3. _____

C **Write, find, and color.** ✏ = with   ✏ = cat

1. with _____

2. cat _____

Read and chant. Then, trace.

♪ Chant

| I |
| I | sleep |
| I | sleep | with my cat | . |

| I | climb | with my cat | . |

Retell **Point, read, and say.**

CAT Cafe

jump

sleep

I _____ with my cat.

walk

run

On Your Own What do you do with your pet?

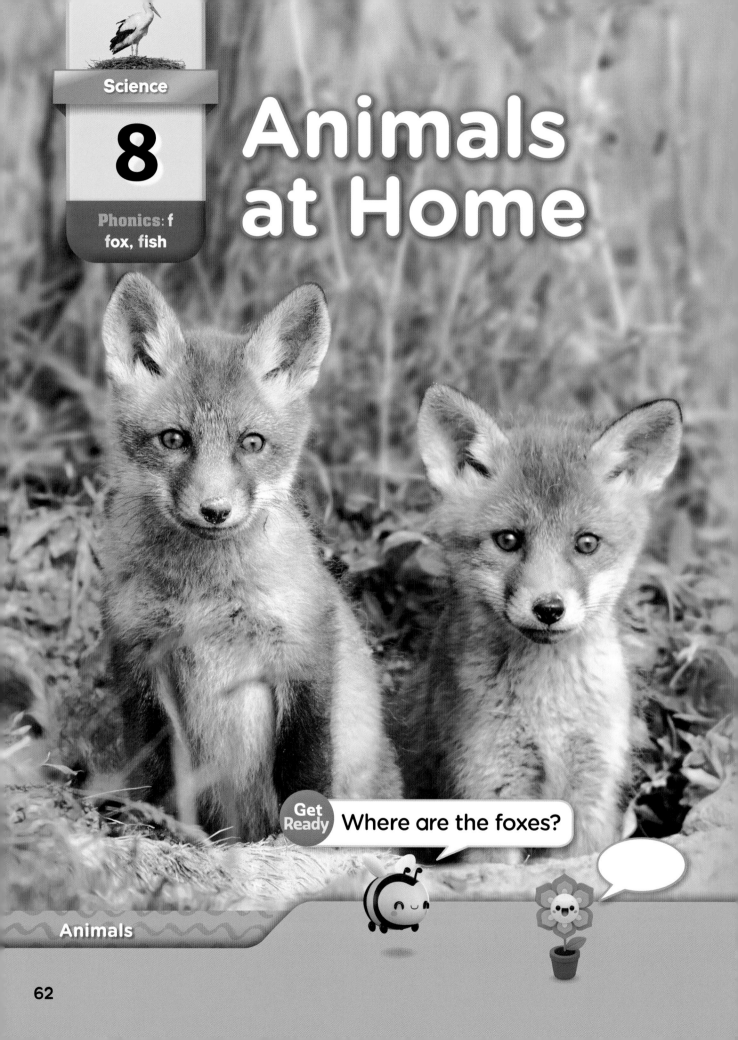

Science

8

Phonics: f
fox, fish

Animals at Home

Get Ready Where are the foxes?

Animals

Word Chant

A **Listen and repeat the words.**

bird

rabbit

crab

fox

fish

Sight Words

at, home

B **Circle the correct words.**

1.

| fox | rabbit |

2.

| bird | fish |

Animals at Home

29 words

What animals are at home?

Animals are at home.
The bird is at home.

Story Song

The rabbit is at home.

Check

Where is the bird's home?

The crab is at home.

The fox is at home.

Check

Where is the crab?

66

The **fish** is at home.

Ff

Phonics Chant

f f f fox
f f f fish
fox fox fox
fish fish fish

Read & Circle

f

rabbit

fox

fish

Reading Comprehension

A Choose the correct answers.

1.

   The _____ is at home.

   ⓐ rabbit   ⓑ fox

2.

   The fish is at home. [Yes] [No]

B Choose and write the correct words.

1.

   | bird |
   | fish |

   _____

2.

   | fox |
   | cat |

   _____

3.

   | crab |
   | rabbit |

   _____

C Write, find, and count.

1. at   _____ ☐

2. home _____ ☐

crab   home
at   the   at
crab   home
the   the   at
home   crab

Build Language

Read and chant. Then, trace.

Chant

The bird

The bird | is

The bird | is | **at home** .

The fish | is | at home .

Retell

Number, read, and say.

① fox　② rabbit　③ bird　④ fish

The _____ is at home.

On Your Own What animals do you see around your house?

Science

9

Phonics: all
tall, small

Zoo Animals

 Get Ready What animal do you like?

Animals

A **Listen and repeat the words.**

♪ Word **Chant**

giraffe

tall

bear

snake

squirrel

Sight Words

these, they

B **Check the correct words.**

1.
☐ bear
☐ giraffe

2.
☐ snake
☐ squirrel

ZOO ANIMALS

28 words

• Focus •
What are the people looking at?

Look at the animals.

These are giraffes.
They are tall.

72

These are bears.

They are big.

Check

Which animals are tall?

These are snakes.
They are long.

all

Phonics Chant

all all all tall
all all all small
tall tall tall
small small small

Write & Read

 t＿ ＿ ＿

 sm＿ ＿ ＿ ＿

74

Find & Draw

these = ◯
they = ▢

These are squirrels.

They are small.

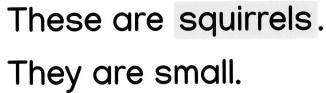

Check

The squirrels are long. [Yes] [No]

Reading Comprehension

A Choose the correct answers.

1.
   ⓐ These are giraffes.
   ⓑ These are squirrels.

2.
   These are bears.
   They are _____ .
   ⓐ small   ⓑ big

B Write the correct words.

1.
   s a n k e
   _____

2.
   g i r f a f e
   _____

3.
   t l a l
   _____

C Write, find, and circle.

1. these _____

2. they _____

t	a	r	g	i	t	a
h	t	h	e	y	h	t
e	n	c	l	f	e	h
s	o	a	j	c	s	e
e	t	h	e	y	e	y
b	m	t	h	e	s	e

Read and chant. Then, trace.

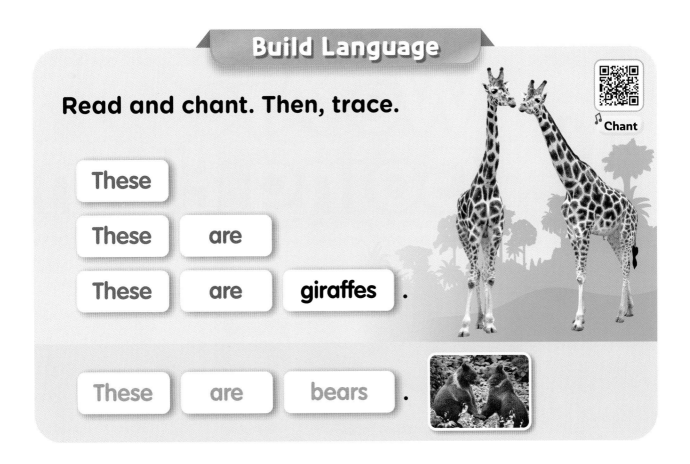

♪ Chant

These

These | are

These | are | **giraffes** .

These | are | bears .

Retell Point, read, and say.

bears

squirrels

giraffes

These are _____ .

snakes

On Your Own What animals can you see at the zoo?

10

Phonics: w
we, way

We Are Going Home

Get Ready What are the kids doing?

Safety and Transportation

A Listen and repeat the words.

 ♫ Word Chant

 way

 bus

 subway

 plane

 ship

Sight Words

on, the

B Circle the correct words.

1.

| way | bus |

2.

| plane | ship |

We Are Going Home

31 words

Where are the people?

We are on our way home.

We are on the bus.

We are on the subway.

🎵 Story Song

Check

Who is on the subway?

We are on the plane.

We are on the ship.

Check

Where are the grandma and grandpa?

82

Now we are at home.

Find & Draw
on = ☆
the = △

Ww

Phonics Chant

w w w we
w w w way
we we we
way way way

Read & Circle

w

 we

 way

 bus

Reading Comprehension

A **Choose the correct answers.**

1. We are on the bus. ⓐ  ⓑ

2.  We are on the
   ⓐ plane .
   ⓑ ship .

B **Choose and write the correct words.**

subway   way   ship

1.

_____

_ _ _ _ _ _ _ _ _ _

2.

_____

_ _ _ _ _ _ _ _ _ _

3.

_____

_ _ _ _ _ _ _ _ _ _

Sight Words

C **Write, find, and color.** 🖍 = on 🖍 = the

1. on _____

_ _ _ _ _ _ _ _ _ _

2. the _____

_ _ _ _ _ _ _ _ _ _

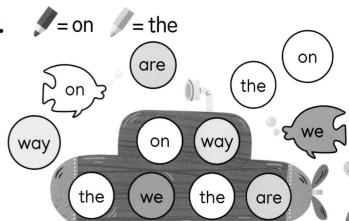

Read and chant. Then, trace.

♪ Chant

| We |
| We | are |
| We | are | on the bus |.

| We | are | on the subway |.

Retell   **Number, read, and say.**

① plane   ② ship   ③ subway   ④ bus

We are on the _____ .

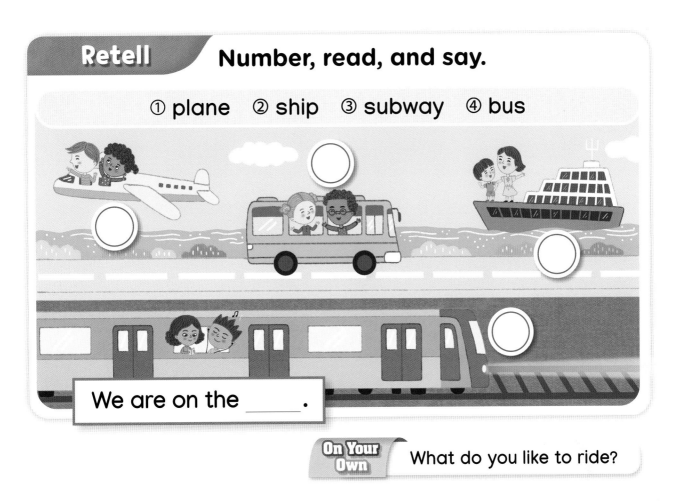

On Your Own   What do you like to ride?

Physical Education

11

Phonics: sk
skate, ski

Ready to Play

Get Ready What is the girl doing?

Safety and Transportation

A **Listen and repeat the words.**

glove

catch

tube

skate

ski

Sight Words

take, let's

B **Check the correct words.**

1.
☐ ski
☐ skate

2.
☐ tube
☐ helmet

Ready to Play

30 words

Focus

What do the children have?

Take the gloves.
Let's catch.

88

Take the tubes.
Let's swim.

Take the hats.
Let's jog.

Check

What do they take to swim?

Take the helmets.
Let's skate.

Take the goggles.
Let's ski.

Check
The children take the goggles
to skate.   Yes   No

We are ready to play.

Find & Draw
take = ◇
let's = ♡

sk **Phonics Chant**

sk sk sk skate
sk sk sk ski
skate skate skate
ski ski ski

Write & Read

 __ __ate

 __ __i

Reading Comprehension

A **Choose the correct answers.**

1.

Let's _____.

ⓐ ski　　ⓑ skate

2.

Take the gloves.　[Yes]　[No]

B **Choose and write the correct words.**

1.

hat

tube

_____

_____

2.

skate

catch

_____

_____

3.

glove

helmet

_____

_____

Sight Words

C **Write, find, and count.**

1. take　-----------------　☐

2. let's　-----------------　☐

let's
ski
let's
jog
let's
take
take
tube let's
swim
take ski
take

92

Read and chant. Then, trace.

♪ Chant

Take the goggles .

Take the goggles . Let's

Take the goggles . Let's ski .

Take the helmets . Let's skate .

Retell Point, read, and say.

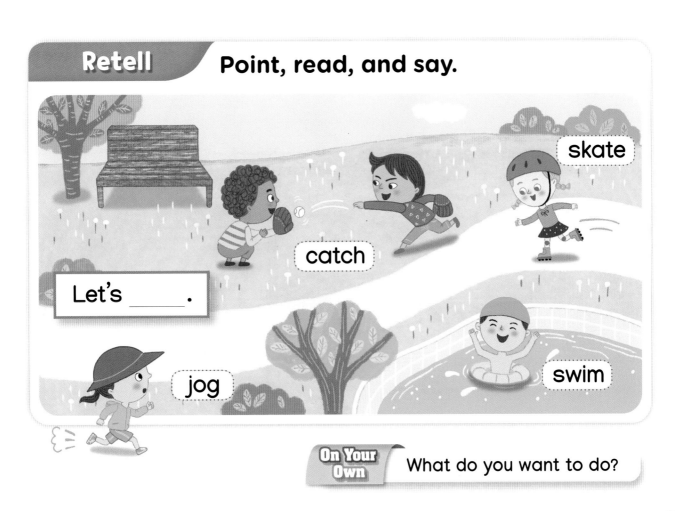

skate

catch

Let's ____ .

jog

swim

On Your Own What do you want to do?

12

Phonics: oo
bedroom, school

Safety Posters

Get Ready What is the girl holding?

Safety and Transportation

♪ **Word Chant**

A **Listen and repeat the words.**

poster

kitchen

bathroom

bedroom

hall

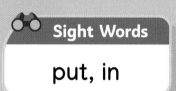
Sight Words

put, in

B **Circle the correct words.**

1.

   kitchen | hall

2.

   bathroom | bedroom

Safety POSTERS

29 words

Look at this poster.

I put it in the kitchen.

96

I put it in the bathroom.

Check

Where is this poster ?

I put it in the bedroom.

Find & Draw

put = ◯
in = ▢

I put it in the school hall.

oo | **Phonics Chant**

oo oo oo bedroom
oo oo oo school
bedroom bedroom bedroom
school school school

Read & Circle

oo bedroom hall school

Reading Comprehension

A **Choose the correct answers.**

1.
   ⓐ I put it in the bedroom.
   ⓑ I put it in the bathroom.

2.
   Look at this poster .
   I put it in the _____.
   ⓐ kitchen   ⓑ school hall

B **Write the correct words.**

1.
   p o t s e r
   _____

2.
   k i t c e h n
   _____

3.
   h l a l
   _____

 Sight Words

C **Write, find, and circle.**

1. put _____

2. in _____

n	o	p	u	t	e	l	m
u	p	j	o	y	l	i	n
i	u	a	i	n	q	o	c
n	t	w	a	p	i	f	e
f	z	p	u	t	w	c	t

Read and chant. Then, trace.

Chant

I

I put it

I put it in the kitchen .

I put it in the bathroom .

Retell   Number, read, and say.

① kitchen   ② bathroom   ③ bedroom   ④ hall

I put it in the ____ .

On Your Own   Where do you want to put a safety poster?

Word List

Unit 1

 eat

 go

 hear

 play

 smell

Unit 2

 clown

 drum

 horn

 parade

 truck

Unit 3

 flower

 pizza

 soap

 sock

 trash

Unit 4

 balloon

 birthday

 bow

 candle

 friend

Unit 5

 cook

 paint

 read

 sing

 swing

Unit 6

 dot

 fur

 hole

 same

 stripe

Unit 7

 climb

 jump

 run

 sleep

 walk

Unit 8

 bird

 crab

 fish

 fox

 rabbit

Unit 9

 bear

 giraffe

 snake

 squirrel

 tall

Unit 10

 bus

 plane

 ship

 subway

 way

Unit 11

 catch

 glove

 skate

 ski

 tube

Unit 12

 bathroom

 bedroom

 hall

 kitchen

 poster

Photo Credits

Student Book

15 Anthony Aneese Totah Jr/Dreamstime **24** lovleah/Getty Images **26** Yellow Dog Productions/Getty Images **27** Fuse/Getty Images **94** Veronica Louro/Shutterstock **96** borisovv/Getty Images **97** lawcain/Getty Images **98** Artazum/Shutterstock **99** Domenica Comfort for Benchmark Education **100** lawcain/Getty Images, Domenica Comfort for Benchmark Education **101** borisovv/Getty Images, lawcain/Getty Images

© shutterstock.com

pp. cover, 2, 3, 4, 6, 7, 11, 13, 14, 20, 21, 22, 23, 24, 25, 27, 28, 29, 30, 31, 32, 36, 37, 38, 39, 40, 41, 42, 43, 44, 45, 46, 47, 52, 53, 54, 55, 60, 61, 62, 63, 64, 65, 66, 67, 69, 70, 71, 74, 76, 77, 78, 79, 83, 84, 85, 86, 87, 92, 93, 94, 95, 96, 98, 99, 100, 101, 102, 103

© gettyimagesbank.com

pp. 2, 3, 4, 7, 11, 12, 13, 14, 15, 19, 20, 21, 23, 28, 29, 31, 35, 36, 37, 39, 40, 41, 42, 43, 44, 45, 46, 47, 51, 52, 54, 55, 58, 61, 62, 63, 64, 65, 67, 68, 69, 71, 74, 76, 77, 78, 79, 83, 84, 87, 89, 91, 92, 95, 97, 99, 100, 101, 102, 103

Workbook

4 Anthony Aneese Totah Jr/Dreamstime **7** lovleah/Getty Images, Fuse/Getty Images, Yellow Dog Productions/Getty Images **25** borisovv/Getty Images, lawcain/Getty Images, Artazum/Shutterstock, Domenica Comfort for Benchmark Education

© shutterstock.com
pp. cover, 2, 6, 7, 8, 10, 11, 14, 16, 17, 18, 20, 22, 24, 25, 26, 27, 28

© gettyimagesbank.com
pp. 2, 4, 6, 7, 8, 10, 11, 12, 14, 16, 17, 18, 20, 22, 24, 25, 26, 27, 28

Benchmark READING™

25 words

Benchmark Reading

WORKBOOK

Starter 2

LEXILE®
BR70L-90L

25 words

Benchmark Reading

Starter 2

WORKBOOK

Benchmark
EDUCATION®
Building Literacy and Language for Life ™

1 We Can Be Together

A Read and write the words twice.

1.  go _____

2.  hear _____

3.  eat _____

4.  smell _____

5.  play _____

B Choose and complete the words. Then, say.

1.
   a
   e
   sm__ll

2.
   e
   i
   tog__ther

C Complete the sight words.

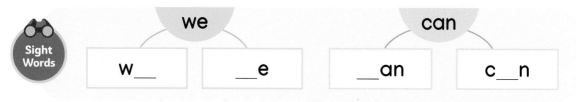

Sight Words

we

w__   __e

can

__an   c__n

Sentence Practice

D Unscramble the words to complete the sentences.

1. We _____

   see.   can

2. We _____

   eat.   can

3. We _____

   love   family.   our

Reading Practice

E Read the sentences and choose the right pictures.

ⓐ We can go.
ⓑ We can hear.
ⓒ We can smell.

1.

2.

3.

② The Parade

Vocabulary Practice

Ⓐ Read and write the words twice.

1.  parade _____

2.  drum _____

3. 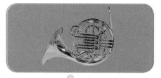 horn _____

4.  clown _____

5.  truck _____

Ⓑ Choose and complete the words. Then, say.

1.
| u |
| i |
dr__m

2.
| e |
| u |
f__n

Ⓒ Complete the sight words.

Sight Words

see
| __ee | s__e |

hear
| hea__ | h__ar |

4

Sentence Practice

D **Unscramble the words to complete the sentences.**

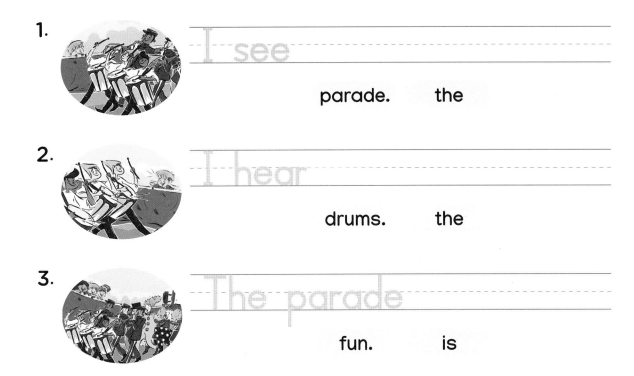

1. I see _____

   parade.   the

2. I hear _____

   drums.   the

3. The parade _____

   fun.   is

Reading Practice

E **Read the sentences and choose the right pictures.**

ⓐ I hear the horns.

ⓑ I see the clowns.

ⓒ I hear the big truck.

1.

2.

3.

3 I Can Smell

A Read and write the words twice.

1.    flower   _____

2.    soap   _____

3.    pizza   _____

4.    sock   _____

5.   trash   _____

B Choose and complete the words. Then, say.

1.
   a / i   tr__sh

2.
   e / a   b__d

C Complete the sight words.

Sight Words

smell   this

sm__ll   s__ell   t__is   th__s

6

D **Unscramble the words to complete the sentences.**

1. I can smell _____

   flower.   this

2. I can smell _____

   this   soap.

3. It _____

   good.   smells

Reading Practice

E **Read the sentences and choose the right pictures.**

ⓐ I can smell this pizza.
ⓑ I can smell this sock.
ⓒ I can smell this trash.

1.

2.

3.

4 My Birthday

A Read and write the words twice.

1.  balloon _____

2.  candle _____

3.  bow _____

4.  friend _____

5.  birthday _____

B Choose and complete the words. Then, say.

1.   b / d __ow

2.  b / f __ox

C Complete the sight words.

Sight Words

I

_____   _____

like

l__ke   lik__

8

Sentence Practice

D **Unscramble the words to complete the sentences.**

1. I like _____

   balloon.   the

2. I open _____

   box.   the

3. I _____

   boat.   the   like

Reading Practice

E **Read the sentences and choose the right pictures.**

ⓐ I like the candle.
ⓑ I like the bow.
ⓒ What a happy birthday!

1.

2.

3.

5 We Are Friends

A Read and write the words twice.

1.  sing _____

2.  swing _____

3.  read _____

4.  paint _____

5.  cook _____

B Choose and complete the words. Then, say.

1.

ing
ink

s__ __ __

2.

eng
ing

sw__ __ __

C Complete the sight words.

Sight Words

are

__re	a__e

together

t__gether	tog__ther

10

Sentence Practice

D **Unscramble the words to complete the sentences.**

1.

We _____

friends.　　are

2.

We _____

read　　together.

3.

We _____

happy.　　are

Reading Practice

E **Read the sentences and choose the right pictures.**

ⓐ We swing together.
ⓑ We paint together.
ⓒ We cook together.

1.

2. (picture)

3.

6 My Mittens

A Read and write the words twice.

1.    dot _____   _____

2. _____   stripe _____   _____

3.    fur _____   _____

4.    hole _____   _____

5.    same _____   _____

B Choose and complete the words. Then, say.

1. 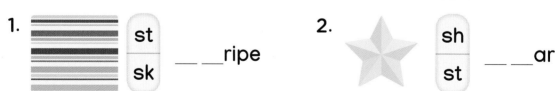 | st / sk | __ __ripe   2. | sh / st | __ __ar

C Complete the sight words.

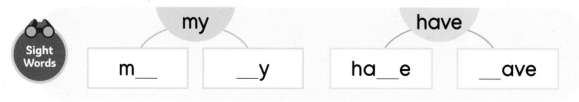

Sight Words

my   m__   __y   have   ha__e   __ave

12

D **Unscramble the words to complete the sentences.**

1. My mittens

stripes.   have

2. My

have   mittens   stars.

3. Look

at   snowman.   the

E **Read the sentences and choose the right pictures.**

ⓐ My mittens have dots.
ⓑ My mittens have holes.
ⓒ We have the same mitten.

1.

2.

3.

7 My Little Cat

A Read and write the words twice.

1.

   run _____ _____

2.

   climb _____ _____

3.

   walk _____ _____

4.

   jump _____ _____

5.

   sleep _____ _____

B Choose and complete the words. Then, say.

1. | c / k | __at

2.  | s / c | __limb

C Complete the sight words.

Sight Words

with

__ith   wi__h

cat

ca__   c__t

14

D **Unscramble the words to complete the sentences.**

1. I run with

      cat.   my

2. I jump

      my   cat.   with

3. I sleep

      cat.   my   with

Reading Practice

E **Read the sentences and choose the right pictures.**

    ⓐ I climb with my cat.
    ⓑ I walk with my cat.
    ⓒ Good night, Kitty!

1.

2.

3.

8 Animals at Home

A Read and write the words twice.

1.  bird

2.  rabbit

3. crab

4. fox

5. fish

B Choose and complete the words. Then, say.

1.  p / f ___ox

2.  f / v ___ish

C Complete the sight words.

Sight Words

at

home

__t   a__   h__me   ho__e

Sentence Practice

D **Unscramble the words to complete the sentences.**

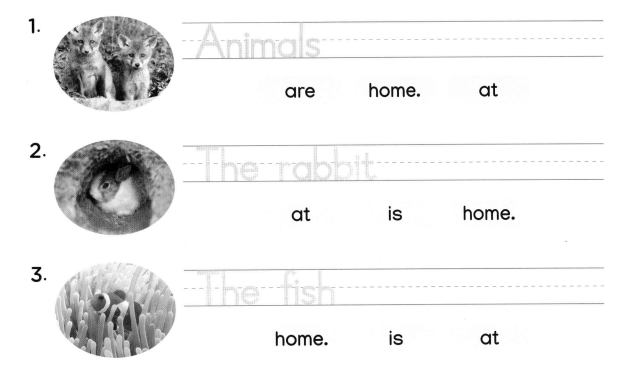

1. Animals _____

      are   home.   at

2. The rabbit _____

      at   is   home.

3. The fish _____

      home.   is   at

Reading Practice

E **Read the sentences and choose the right pictures.**

ⓐ The bird is at home.
ⓑ The crab is at home.
ⓒ The fox is at home.

1.

2.

3.

⑨ Zoo Animals

Vocabulary Practice

A Read and write the words twice.

1.  giraffe _____

2.  tall _____

3.  bear _____

4.  snake _____

5.  squirrel _____

B Choose and complete the words. Then, say.

1.   all / ill   t__ __ __

2.   all / ing   sm__ __ __

C Complete the sight words.

Sight Words

these

| t__ese | the__e |

they

| th__y | t__ey |

18

D **Unscramble the words to complete the sentences.**

1.

   These _____

   are   giraffes.

2. These _____

   snakes.   are

3. They _____

   small.   are

Reading Practice

E **Read the sentences and choose the right pictures.**

> ⓐ These are bears. They are big.
> ⓑ These are snakes. They are long.
> ⓒ These are squirrels. They are small.

1.

2.

3.

10 We Are Going Home

Vocabulary Practice

A Read and write the words twice.

1.  way _____ _____

2.  bus _____ _____

3.  subway _____ _____

4.  plane _____ _____

5.  ship _____ _____

B Choose and complete the words. Then, say.

1.
s
w
__e

2.
p
w
__ay

C Complete the sight words.

Sight Words

on

__n   o__

the

t__e   __he

20

Sentence Practice

D Unscramble the words to complete the sentences.

1.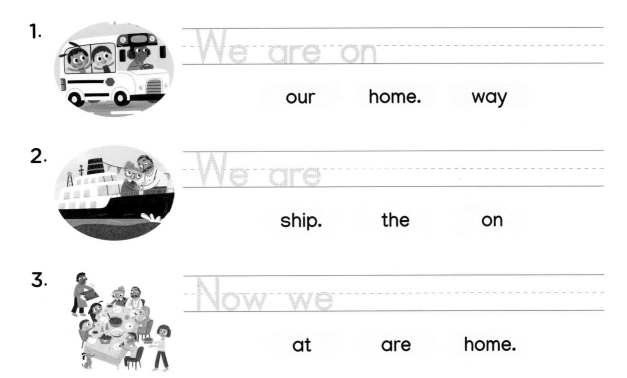

   We are on _____

   our   home.   way

2. We are _____

   ship.   the   on

3. Now we _____

   at   are   home.

Reading Practice

E Read the sentences and choose the right pictures.

ⓐ We are on the bus.
ⓑ We are on the subway.
ⓒ We are on the plane.

1.

2.

3.

11 Ready to Play

Vocabulary Practice

A Read and write the words twice.

1.  glove _____

2.  catch _____

3.  tube _____

4.  skate _____

5.  ski _____

B Choose and complete the words. Then, say.

1.
sl / sk   __ __ate

2.
sk / st   __ __i

C Complete the sight words.

 Sight Words

take

__ake   ta__e

let's

let'__   l__t's

22

Sentence Practice

D Unscramble the words to complete the sentences.

1. 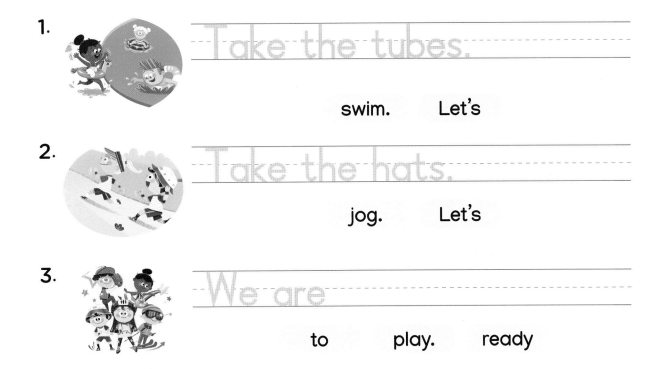 Take the tubes.

   swim.   Let's

2. Take the hats.

   jog.   Let's

3. We are

   to   play.   ready

Reading Practice

E Read the sentences and choose the right pictures.

ⓐ Take the gloves. Let's catch.
ⓑ Take the helmets. Let's skate.
ⓒ Take the goggles. Let's ski.

1.

2.

3.

12 Safety Posters

A Read and write the words twice.

1.  poster

2.  kitchen

3.  bathroom

4.  bedroom

5.  hall

B Choose and complete the words. Then, say.

1.
   oo / au   bedr__ __m

2.
   ee / oo   sch__ __l

C Complete the sight words.

Sight Words

put   __ut   p__t

in   i__   __n

Sentence Practice

D Unscramble the words to complete the sentences.

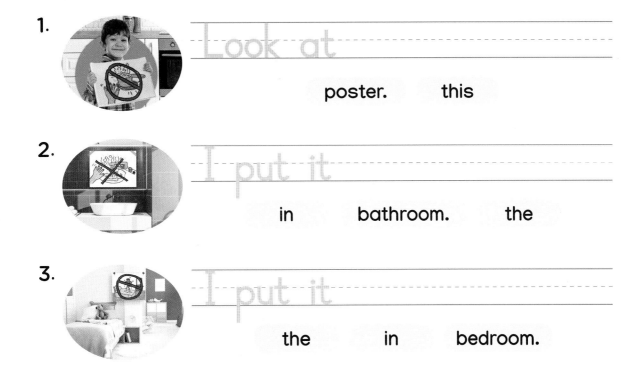

1. Look at _____

   poster.   this

2. I put it _____

   in   bathroom.   the

3. I put it _____

   the   in   bedroom.

Reading Practice

E Read the sentences and choose the right pictures.

ⓐ I put it in the kitchen.
ⓑ I put it in the bathroom.
ⓒ I put it in the school hall.

1.

2.

3.

• Make your own picture dictionary.

Unit 1

Unit 2

Unit 3

Unit 4

Unit 5

_____
_____
_____

_____
_____
_____

_____
_____
_____

_____
_____
_____

_____
_____
_____

Unit 6

_____
_____
_____

_____
_____
_____

_____
_____
_____

_____
_____
_____

_____
_____
_____

Unit 7

_____
_____
_____

_____
_____
_____

_____
_____
_____

_____
_____
_____

_____
_____
_____

Unit 8

_____
_____
_____

_____
_____
_____

_____
_____
_____

_____
_____
_____

_____
_____
_____

Unit 9

Unit 10

Unit 11

Unit 12

Benchmark Reading

Starter 2

 LEXILE® BR70L–90L

Benchmark Reading is a theme-based, comprehensive seven-level reading series for English language learners. This series includes a wide range of informative theme-based subjects, such as social studies, science, math, literature, physical education, and art. Each reading passage is supported by a set of reading activities to help improve learners' understanding of the texts and to develop their critical and comprehensive reading skills. The primary objective of the series is to enable learners to develop various skills so that they can read and understand complex texts.

Features

- Theme-based authentic texts related to learners' experiences
- A good balance of fiction and nonfiction texts
- Well-designed comprehension questions and vocabulary tasks
- Various activities to reinforce phonics and sight word skills
- Engaging word/phonics/build language chants, story songs, and activities for language building
- Retell and On Your Own activities for learners to express what they have learned
- Colorful illustrations and visual aids that engage learners

Components

- Student Book / Workbook
- Teachers' Guide / E-book
- Online Resources: **www.ybmbooksam.com**
  MP3 Files / Answer Keys / Word Lists & Tests / Tests / Worksheets / Presentation Slides / Dictations / Translations

Benchmark Reading Starter

 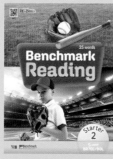 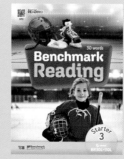

(20–25 words)　　(25–30 words)　　(30–35 words)

이투스북

Word 초등
∞ master

BASIC Mini

QR 바로듣기가 가능한
예쁘고 알찬 미니북으로
영단어를 복습하세요.

마스터 시리즈
900만

빈출어휘 **1위**

온&오프 듀얼
영단어 학습앱

Word 초등
∞ master

BASIC

| Mini |

작고 편리한 미니북 활용하기

1 **복습할 때 활용하세요**
단어 학습 후 약 1주일 뒤, 잊은 단어는 없는지 미니북으로 확인해 보세요.

2 **QR로 발음도 들어봐요**
정확한 발음 확인을 위해 QR 듣기도 활용하여 다시 한 번 발음을 들어 보세요.

3 **잊은 단어가 있다면 다시 꼼꼼하게 암기해요**
잊은 단어가 있다면 체크하여 뜻과 철자, 발음을 꼼꼼하게 외워요.

4 **주기적으로 활용하며 체크하는 것도 좋아요**
반복을 통해 단어를 완벽하게 기억하도록, 미니북으로 주기적으로 활용하며
체크해 보세요.

DAY 01 **Body** 몸

완료했으면 ✓ 표시 하세요.

철자/뜻 암기 발음 듣기

001 **body** 몸

002 **head** 머리

003 **face** 얼굴

004 **eye** 눈

005 **nose** 코

複습 날짜　　월　　일

완료했으면 ✔ 표시 하세요.

철자/뜻 암기　발음 듣기

006

mouth　　입

007

tooth　　이, 이빨

008

neck　　목

009

hand　　손

010

foot　　발

Senses & Feelings 감각과 감정

완료했으면 ✔ 표시 하세요.

철자/뜻 암기   발음 듣기

011 **see** 보다

012 **listen** 듣다

013 **smell** ~한 냄새가 나다

014 **taste** 맛이 ~하다

015 **touch** 만지다

• Word master 초등 BASIC

완료했으면 ✓ 표시 하세요.

철자/뜻 암기   발음 듣기

016

feel   느끼다

017

sad   슬픈

018

happy   행복한

019

angry   화난

020

proud   자랑스러운

Personality 성격

021

kind   친절한

022

shy   수줍어하는

023

funny   재미있는

024

clever   영리한,
똑똑한

025

brave   용감한

완료했으면 ✓ 표시 하세요.

철자/뜻 암기　발음 듣기

026

lazy　　　　게으른

027

wise　　　　지혜로운,
현명한

028

honest　　　정직한

029

rude　　　　예의 없는,
버릇없는

030

polite　　　예의 바른,
공손한

완료했으면 ✔ 표시 하세요.

철자/뜻 암기	발음 듣기

031 **sleep** (잠을) **자다**

032 **wake up** (잠에서) **깨다**

033 **wash** 씻다

034 **eat** 먹다

035 **go** 가다

완료했으면 ✓ 표시 하세요.

철자/뜻 암기　발음 듣기

036

 **come** 오다

037

 **play**
1 **놀다**
2 (게임, 운동 등을) **하다**
3 (악기를) **연주하다**

038

 talk 말하다

039

 sit 앉다

040

 stand 서다

Health 건강

완료했으면 ✔ 표시 하세요.

철자/뜻 암기   발음 듣기

041

weak 약한, 힘이 없는

042

strong 튼튼한, 힘센

043

sick 아픈

044

healthy 건강한

045

tired 피곤한

완료했으면 ✓ 표시 하세요.

철자/뜻 암기　　발음 듣기

046

illness　　병

047

pain　　아픔, 고통

048

cough　　기침하다

049

pill　　알약

050

hospital　　병원

DAY 06 **Family** 가족

완료했으면 ✓ 표시 하세요.

철자/뜻 암기 발음 듣기

051
father
(= dad)
아버지 (= 아빠)

052
mother
(= mom)
어머니 (= 엄마)

053
grandfather
할아버지

054
grandmother
할머니

055
brother
형, 오빠, 남동생

완료했으면 ✓ 표시 하세요.

철자/뜻 암기   발음 듣기

056  **sister** 언니, 누나, 여동생

057  **son** 아들

058  **daughter** 딸

059  **uncle** (외)삼촌, 고모부, 이모부

060  **aunt** 고모, 이모, (외)숙모

People 사람들

완료했으면 ✔ 표시 하세요.

철자/뜻 암기   발음 듣기

061 **baby** 아기

062 **kid** 아이

063 **boy** 소년,
남자아이

064 **girl** 소녀,
여자아이

065 **friend** 친구

066

man 남자

067

woman 여자

068

couple
1 부부, 남녀
2 두 개,
　두 사람

069

meet 만나다

070

help 돕다

DAY 08 **Jobs** 직업

완료했으면 ✓ 표시 하세요.

철자/뜻 암기 ｜ 발음 듣기

071  **future** 미래, 장래

072 **dream** 꿈, 꿈을 꾸다

073 **teacher** 교사, 선생님

074 **firefighter** 소방관

075 **singer** 가수

완료했으면 ✔ 표시 하세요.

철자/뜻 암기   발음 듣기

076   **dancer**   무용수, 댄서

077   **doctor**   의사

078   **nurse**   간호사

079   **pianist**   피아니스트

080   **farmer**   농부

Appearance 생김새

완료했으면 ✓ 표시 하세요.

철자/뜻 암기   발음 듣기

081 **tall** 키가 큰

082 **short**
1 키가 작은
2 (길이가) 짧은

083 **fat** 뚱뚱한

084 **slim** 날씬한

085 **young** 젊은, 어린

완료했으면 ✔표시 하세요.

철자/뜻 암기   발음 듣기

old

1 늙은
2 나이가 ~인

cute

귀여운

beautiful

아름다운

ugly

못생긴

curly

곱슬곱슬한

Clothes 옷

완료했으면 ✓ 표시 하세요.

철자/뜻 암기 발음 듣기

091

hat 모자

092

shirt 셔츠

093

sweater 스웨터

094

skirt 치마

095

pants 1 바지 2 팬티

완료했으면 ✔ 표시 하세요.
철자/뜻 암기 　발음 듣기

096

jacket 　　재킷

097

coat 　　코트, 외투

098

sock 　　양말

099

shoe 　　신발

100

wear 　　입고 있다

DAY 11 **Food** 음식

철자/뜻 암기 발음 듣기

101
 food 음식

102
 water 물

103
 milk 우유

104
 bread 빵

105
 apple 사과

완료했으면 ✓ 표시 하세요.

철자/뜻 암기   발음 듣기

106 **egg**   달걀

107 **cake**   케이크

108 **full**
1 배부른
2 가득 찬

109 **hungry**   배고픈

110 **drink**
1 마시다
2 음료

완료했으면 ✓ 표시 하세요.

철자/뜻 암기 | 발음 듣기

111 **car** 자동차, 차

112 **bus** 버스

113 **ship** 배, 선박

114 **subway** 지하철

115  **train** 기차

완료했으면 ✓ 표시 하세요.

철자/뜻 암기   발음 듣기

116

airplane   비행기

117

bicycle
(= bike)   자전거

118

walk   걷다

119

take   1 (교통수단을)
타다
2 (사진을) **찍다**

120

stop   1 **멈추다**
2 **정류장**

Color & Shape 색과 모양

완료했으면 ✓ 표시 하세요.

철자/뜻 암기   발음 듣기

121	**color**	색깔
122	**red**	빨간색
123	**blue**	파란색
124	**yellow**	노란색
125	**green**	초록색

완료했으면 ✔ 표시 하세요.

철자/뜻 암기   발음 듣기

126

white   흰색

127

black   검정색

128

circle   원, 동그라미

129

triangle   삼각형

130

square   정사각형

DAY 14 Numbers 숫자

완료했으면 ✔ 표시 하세요.

철자/뜻 암기 발음 듣기

131 **one** 하나, 1

132 **two** 둘, 2

133 **three** 셋, 3

134 **four** 넷, 4

135 **five** 다섯, 5

136  **six** 여섯, 6

137 **seven** 일곱, 7

138 **eight** 여덟, 8

139 **nine** 아홉, 9

140  **ten** 열, 10

Location & Direction 위치와 방향

완료했으면 ✓ 표시 하세요.

철자/뜻 암기 발음 듣기

141 **left** 왼쪽,
왼쪽으로

142 **right** 오른쪽,
오른쪽으로

143 **up** 위쪽에

144 **down** 아래에

145 **front** 앞쪽에

완료했으면 ✓표시 하세요.

철자/뜻 암기　발음 듣기

146

behind
뒤에

147

inside
(~의) 안에,
~ 안으로

148

outside
(~의) 밖에,
~ 밖으로

149

near
가까운,
가까이에

150

far
먼, 멀리에

완료했으면 ✓ 표시 하세요.

철자/뜻 암기   발음 듣기

151

Sunday   일요일

152

Monday   월요일

153

Tuesday   화요일

154

Wednesday   수요일

155

Thursday   목요일

156 **Friday** 금요일

157 **Saturday** 토요일

158 **morning** 아침, 오전

159 **afternoon** 오후

160 **night** 밤, 야간

House 1 집

161

 house　　　집, 주택

162

 door　　　문

163

 bell　　　벨, 초인종

164

 room　　　방

165

 garden　　　정원

완료했으면 ✓ 표시 하세요.

철자/뜻 암기 　발음 듣기

166

roof 　　지붕

167

wall 　　벽

168

floor 　　바닥

169

window 　　창문

170

stairs 　　계단

House 2 집

완료했으면 ✓ 표시 하세요.

철자/뜻 암기 발음 듣기

171

bed 침대

172

lamp 램프, 등

173

chair 의자

174

table 탁자, 테이블

175

desk 책상

완료했으면 ✓ 표시 하세요.

철자/뜻 암기　발음 듣기

176

sofa　소파

177

clock　시계

178

towel　수건

179

soap　비누

180

mirror　거울

DAY 19 **School 1** 학교

철자/뜻 암기 발음 듣기

181 **study** 공부하다

182 **teach** 가르치다

183 **class**
1 학급, 반
2 수업

184 **read** 읽다

185 **write** 쓰다

완료했으면 ✓ 표시 하세요.
철자/뜻 암기 발음 듣기

186

homework 숙제

187

prize 상, 상품

188

student 학생

189

classroom 교실

190

playground 운동장

School 2 학교

191

book 책

192

eraser 지우개

193

pencil 연필

194

scissors 가위

195

pen 펜

완료했으면 ✔ 표시 하세요.

철자/뜻 암기　발음 듣기

196

bag　　가방

197

ruler　　자

198

glue　　풀

199

textbook　　교과서

200

notebook　　공책

201
buy
사다,
구입하다

202
sell
팔다

203
price
가격

204
shop
1 가게, 상점
2 쇼핑하다

205
money
돈

복습 날짜   월   일

완료했으면 ✓ 표시 하세요.

철자/뜻 암기   발음 듣기

206

coin

동전

207

sale

1 판매
2 세일, 할인
  판매

208

change

1 바꾸다
2 잔돈

209

choose

선택하다,
고르다

210

store

가게, 상점

완료했으면 ✓ 표시 하세요.

철자/뜻 암기   발음 듣기

211  **zoo** 동물원

212 **market** 시장

213 **farm** 농장

214 **park** 공원

215 **bank** 은행

완료했으면 ✓ 표시 하세요.

철자/뜻 암기   발음 듣기

216 **airport** 공항

217 **church** 교회

218 **library** 도서관

219 **museum** 박물관

220 **restaurant** 식당

DAY 23 Weather 날씨

완료했으면 ✔ 표시 하세요.

철자/뜻 암기　발음 듣기

221 **cold**
1 추운, 차가운
2 감기

222 **hot**
더운, 뜨거운

223 **cool**
시원한

224 **warm**
따뜻한

225 **windy**
바람 부는

48　Word master 초등 BASIC

완료했으면 ✔ 표시 하세요.

철자/뜻 암기　발음 듣기

226

sunny 화창한

227

cloudy 흐린

228

rainy 비가 오는

229

snowy 눈이 오는

230

rainbow 무지개

Season 계절

완료했으면 ✓ 표시 하세요.

철자/뜻 암기 발음 듣기

231 **spring** 봄

232 **summer** 여름

233 **fall** 가을

234  **winter** 겨울

235 **air** 공기, 대기

완료했으면 ✓ 표시 하세요.

철자/뜻 암기　　발음 듣기

236

wind　　　　바람

237

ice　　　　얼음

238

melt　　　　녹다, 녹이다

239

dry　　　　마른, 건조한

240

wet　　　　젖은, 습한

241

ant 　개미

242

cat 　고양이

243

dog 　개

244

pig 　돼지

245

snake 　뱀

완료했으면 ✓ 표시 하세요.

철자/뜻 암기　발음 듣기

246

bear　　　곰

247

duck　　　오리

248

lion　　　사자

249

bat　　　박쥐

250

fish　　　물고기

DAY 26 Earth 지구

251

sky 하늘

252

sea 바다

253

land 육지, 땅

254

tree 나무

255

flower 꽃

완료했으면 ✓ 표시 하세요.

철자/뜻 암기   발음 듣기

256

field   들판

257

river   강

258

lake   호수

259

cloud   구름

260

mountain   산

완료했으면 ✔ 표시 하세요.

철자/뜻 암기 | 발음 듣기

261 **big** 큰

262  **small** 작은

263 **long** 긴

264 **story** 이야기

265 **king** 왕

완료했으면 ✓ 표시 하세요.

철자/뜻 암기   발음 듣기

266

family   가족

267

give   주다

268

have   1 가지다
                   2 먹다, 마시다

269

wait   기다리다

270

catch   잡다

완료했으면 ✓ 표시 하세요.

철자/뜻 암기 ┃ 발음 듣기

271

cut 자르다

272

run 뛰다, 달리다

273

make 만들다

274

do 하다

275

name 이름

완료했으면 ✓ 표시 하세요.

철자/뜻 암기　발음 듣기

276

age　　　　나이

277

deep　　　　깊은

278

hard　　　　1 열심히
　　　　　　　　2 단단한

279

bottle　　　병

280
begin　　　시작하다

완료했으면 ✔ 표시 하세요.

철자/뜻 암기　발음 듣기

281

low　　　　낮은, 낮게

282

high　　　　높은, 높이

283

top　　　　맨 위, 꼭대기

284

open　　　　열다

285

close　　　　닫다

완료했으면 ✓ 표시 하세요.

철자/뜻 암기 | 발음 듣기

286 **burn** 1 타다 2 데다

287 **hate** 싫어하다,
미워하다

288 **start** 시작하다

289 **bite** 물다

290 **dirty** 더러운

완료했으면 ✔ 표시 하세요.
철자/뜻 암기   발음 듣기

291

week   주, 일주일

292

month   달, 월

293

year   1 해, 년
                  2 나이, ~살

294

new   새로운

295

today   오늘

완료했으면 ✓ 표시 하세요.

철자/뜻 암기　　발음 듣기

296

fire

화재, 불

297

turn

돌다, 돌리다

298

line

1 줄, 선
2 줄을 서다

299

dark

어두운

300

lie

1 누워 있다
2 거짓말,
　거짓말하다